Easy Italian

SAVEUR

Tom Nicolosi (right), owner of DiNic's Roast Pork in Philadelphia, and his son, Joe Nicolosi, tuck into pulled pork Italiano sandwiches (for a recipe, see page 85).

Easy Italian

37 Classic Recipes

SAVEUR

BY THE EDITORS OF SAVEUR MAGAZINE

weldon**owen**

Onlookers watch a chef at a restaurant in New York City cooking spaghetti, circa 1937.

TABLE OF CONTENTS

At a pasticceria in Sicily, a local appraises
Easter breads and other specialties.

INTRODUCTION

It's no wonder we're always cooking Italian. Many of Italy's most satisfying foods are also some of the world's simplest to prepare. Take spaghetti carbonara, that luscious Roman pasta dish: It's made with little more than parmigiano-reggiano, eggs, cured pork, and a liberal dose of black pepper, tossed together just before serving. Or savory veal shanks braised in wine until they're fall-off-the-bone tender: The meal virtually cooks itself. Italian food may be inherently easy, but that doesn't make it any less brilliant. Its success rests in quality ingredients and spare tehniques that allow flavors to shine. A quick sauté of escarole is vibrant with anchovies and plenty of garlic; day-old bread is transformed into a beautiful salad thanks to ripe tomatoes, fresh herbs, and olive oil. This book features the regional dishes that are in heaviest rotation in Italian home kitchens, from Emilia-Romagna's buttery pastas to Tuscany's creamy polentas to Sicily's sun-sweetened tomato sauces. Consider these recipes your culinary road map—complete with cooking tips, wine pairings, serving suggestions, and information about Italian food's history and lore—to la dolce vita.

—THE EDITORS

Zia ("Aunt") Pina at her restaurant, which shares her name, near the Vucciria market in Palermo, Sicily.

Starters

*Whether it's an array of cold dishes or
a simple plate of polenta, these classic
first courses are as simple to prepare
as they are delicious to eat.*

SWEET AND SOUR EGGPLANT RELISH

Caponata

SERVES 6–8

This sumptuous, sweet-tart Sicilian relish is wonderful served alongside grilled fish or steak, and it makes a great antipasto when spooned atop crostini.

3	cups olive oil
2	lbs. eggplant, cut into 1-inch cubes
1	large yellow onion, chopped
1	rib celery, roughly chopped
	Kosher salt and ground black pepper, to taste
3	tbsp. tomato paste, thinned with ¼ cup water
1	cup canned whole peeled tomatoes in juice, crushed
6	oz. green olives, pitted and roughly chopped
½	cup white wine vinegar
½	cup golden raisins
¼	cup salt-packed capers, rinsed and drained
3	tbsp. sugar
2	tbsp. finely grated unsweetened chocolate
½	cup finely shredded basil
2	tbsp. pine nuts

1 Heat the oil in a 12-inch skillet over medium-high heat. Working in batches, add the eggplant and fry, tossing occasionally, until browned, 3–4 minutes. Using a slotted spoon, transfer the eggplant to a large bowl; set aside. Pour off all but ¼ cup oil, and reserve for another use.

2 Return the skillet to the heat, add the onion and celery, and season with salt and pepper; cook, stirring often, until the onion and celery begin to brown, 10 minutes. Reduce the heat to medium, and add the tomato paste and cook, stirring, until the tomato paste is caramelized and almost evaporated, 1–2 minutes. Add the crushed tomatoes and continue cooking for 10 minutes. Stir in the olives, vinegar, raisins, capers, sugar, and chocolate, and cook, stirring occasionally, until thickened, about 15 minutes. Transfer to the bowl with the eggplant, along with the basil and pine nuts, and mix together. Season with salt and pepper, and let cool to room temperature before serving.

Cooking Note *Chocolate is a traditional ingredient that adds a bittersweet edge, but the caponata is just as delicious without it.*

SAUTÉED GREENS

Verdure in Padella

SERVES 4

For this flavorful side dish, escarole is cooked in anchovy-and-garlic-infused oil. Like most bitter greens, escarole benefits from a quick initial blanching, which mellows its flavor and turns it a vibrant green.

Kosher salt, to taste

2 large heads escarole, tough outer leaves discarded, inner leaves, roughly chopped, washed, drained, and dried

5 tbsp. extra-virgin olive oil

1 tsp. crushed red chile flakes

6 garlic cloves, thinly sliced crosswise

3 oil-packed anchovy fillets, chopped

Freshly ground black pepper, to taste

2 tbsp. fresh lemon juice

1 Bring an 8-qt. pot of salted water to a boil. Add the escarole and cook, stirring occasionally, until tender, about 3 minutes. Drain the escarole and transfer to a bowl. Heat 3 tbsp. oil in a 12-inch skillet over medium heat. Add the chile flakes, garlic, and anchovies and cook, stirring frequently, until the garlic is golden brown, about 4 minutes. Increase the heat to medium-high. Add the escarole and cook, tossing frequently with tongs, until just wilted, about 3 minutes. Season the escarole with salt and pepper and toss with lemon juice. Divide the greens among plates and drizzle with the remaining oil.

Cooking Note *This anchovy- and garlic-spiked sauté works just as well with other bitter, leafy greens, such as dandelion and collard greens.*

CREAMY POLENTA WITH MUSHROOMS AND SPINACH

Polenta con Funghi e Spinaci

SERVES 6

Slow-simmered cornmeal, enriched with butter and cheese, is a staple in northern Italy, where it's topped with everything from vegetable sautés—like the spinach and mushrooms in this recipe—to hearty meat sauces.

1 cup yellow or white coarse-grain polenta or cornmeal (pictured below)

½ cup grated parmigiano-reggiano

3 tbsp. unsalted butter

2 tbsp. mascarpone cheese

Kosher salt and freshly ground black pepper, to taste

5 tbsp. extra-virgin olive oil

3 cloves garlic, smashed

1 medium yellow onion, halved lengthwise and thinly sliced

½ lb. spinach, trimmed

½ lb. cremini mushrooms, stemmed and cut into sixths

1 tsp. finely chopped fresh thyme leaves

2 tbsp. roughly chopped flat-leaf parsley leaves

1 Bring 6 cups of water to a boil in a 4-qt. heavy-bottomed saucepan. Gradually whisk in the polenta, reduce the heat to low, and cook, whisking frequently, until the polenta is tender and thick, about 1 hour (whisk in a little water if the polenta seems dry). Whisk in ¼ cup parmigiano, 2 tbsp. butter, and the mascarpone, and season the polenta with salt and pepper. Cover and keep warm.

2 Meanwhile, heat 3 tbsp. olive oil in a 12-inch skillet over medium-high heat. Add the garlic and onion and cook, stirring occasionally, until soft and golden brown, about 12 minutes. Add the spinach and cook, stirring frequently, until wilted, about 3 minutes. Season with salt and pepper and transfer the spinach mixture to a bowl; set aside. Heat the remaining oil over medium-high heat. Add the mushrooms and cook, stirring occasionally, until golden and tender, about 6 minutes. Add the thyme and remaining butter and season with salt and pepper; cook, stirring frequently, until the flavors meld, about 1 more minute. Remove from the heat and set aside.

3 Pour the polenta into a serving dish and top it with the spinach and mushrooms. Sprinkle the remaining parmigiano and the parsley over the top.

Cooking Note *You can replace the mascarpone in this recipe with any soft, creamy cheese you have on hand, such as ricotta or gorgonzola dolce.*

PESTO FOCACCIA

SERVES 12-16

This version of Liguria's famed focaccia, topped with pesto, tomatoes, olives, and onions, comes from Biagio Settepani, executive pastry chef and co-owner of Pasticceria Bruno in New York City.

FOR THE PESTO:

1¼	cups packed basil leaves
¼	cup olive oil
¼	cup grated parmigiano-reggiano
2	tbsp. minced sun-dried tomatoes in oil
2	tbsp. pine nuts
1	clove garlic, minced
	Kosher salt and ground black pepper, to taste

FOR THE FOCACCIA:

1	tbsp. active dry yeast
⅓	cup boiled, mashed potatoes
1	tbsp. melted butter
1	tbsp. lager beer
1	tbsp. kosher salt
5½	cups wheat flour
12	kalamata olives, pitted and halved
10	cherry tomatoes, halved
½	small red onion, sliced
½	cup grated parmigiano-reggiano
½	cup packed basil leaves

1 Make the pesto: Process the basil, oil, parmigiano, tomatoes, nuts, garlic, and salt and pepper in a food processor until smooth, and then refrigerate.

2 Make the focaccia: In the bowl of a stand mixer fitted with a dough hook, combine the yeast and 2 cups of water heated to 115°F; let sit until foamy, about 10 minutes. In a bowl, stir together the potatoes, butter, beer, and salt until smooth; add to the yeast mixture and whisk until smooth. Add the flour and mix on medium speed until a dough forms. Increase the speed to medium-high and knead until the dough is smooth, about 8 minutes. Cover the bowl with plastic wrap and let the dough rise until it has tripled in volume, about 3 hours.

3 Transfer the dough to a greased 13-x-18-inch rimmed baking sheet and, using your fingers, spread the dough until it completely covers the bottom. Using your hands, spread pesto evenly over the dough, and then scatter olives, tomatoes, and onion over the pesto. Sprinkle parmigiano over the top of the dough and, using your fingertips, press the dough all over to form dimples. Let sit, uncovered, until puffed, about 45 minutes.

4 Heat the oven to 400°F. Bake the focaccia until its edges are golden brown and the dough is cooked through, about 20 minutes. Let cool for 10 minutes and then scatter basil leaves over the top; cut into squares and serve.

Cooking Note *Make an extra batch of the pesto and store it in the refrigerator for up to one week to toss with pasta or vegetables, or to stir into chicken soup.*

A waitress transcribes the day's specials at restaurant

OUR DAILY BREAD

We have to confess: There are days when we would happily forgo multicourse meals in favor of eating nothing but bruschetta (pronounced brew-SKET-ta, from the Italian verb bruscare, "to toast"). This toasted bread antipasto is easy to prepare, yet it can rival the finest pizza. Start with excellent bread (a thick-crusted variety with a chewy crumb is best); crisp it up on the grill over smoldering charcoal, which gives it a smoky flavor, or simply bake it at 300 degrees Fahrenheit until it's nicely charred; rub it down with fresh garlic (we love the juicy hard-neck kind with brawny cloves); top with an array of seasonal vegetables, cheeses, cured meats, and fish; then drench it in green olive oil, and season with salt and pepper. Italian cooks often serve bruschetta with chopped tomatoes tossed with fresh basil; cannellini beans mixed with fresh rosemary; black olives mashed into a paste along with chile flakes; capers and anchovies, right out of the jar; a spoonful of ricotta strewn with grated lemon zest and torn fresh mint; shaved mushrooms with slivers of pecorino; soft gorgonzola dolce with a schmear of pear preserves or mostarda. The possibilities are almost infinite.

BAKED CLAMS

SERVES 6

Plump clams baked with an herb-flecked bread crumb topping are an Italian-American restaurant favorite that are easy to make at home. The sauce more or less makes itself in the pan as the clams' liquor, butter, and white wine simmer together.

36	littleneck clams, top shells removed, juices reserved in a bowl
1½	cups bread crumbs
¼	cup finely chopped flat-leaf parsley, plus more to garnish
6	tbsp. extra-virgin olive oil
1½	tbsp. crushed red chile flakes
2	tsp. dried oregano
	Kosher salt and ground black pepper, to taste
9	tbsp. unsalted butter, each tablespoon cut into 4 cubes
½	cup white wine
	Lemon wedges, for serving

1 Heat the oven to 425°F. Place the clams on a rimmed baking sheet; set aside. Toss the bread crumbs, parsley, oil, chile flakes, oregano, and salt and pepper in a bowl; spoon the mixture evenly over the clams. Top each stuffed clam with a cube of butter. Pour the reserved clam juices and the wine around the clams on the baking sheet, and bake until the stuffing is golden brown, about 16 minutes.

2 To serve, place the stuffed clams on a serving platter and pour the pan juices around the clams. Sprinkle with parsley and serve them with lemon wedges.

Wine Pairing *These briny, buttery clams are a perfect match for a bright, young verdicchio such as Castelli di Jesi DOC.*

SPRING RISOTTO

Risi e Bisi

SERVES 4

This creamy risotto appears on Venetian tables late each spring, when gardens are yielding the first peas of the year—though it's delicious made with frozen peas, too. Pancetta sautéed in butter provides a deep savory note that runs through the entire dish.

6   cups chicken stock

4   tbsp. unsalted butter

2   oz. pancetta, finely chopped

1   small yellow onion, minced

2   tbsp extra-virgin olive oil

1⅓ cups risotto rice

     Kosher salt and freshly ground black pepper, to taste

2   lbs. fresh or frozen green peas

½   bunch flat-leaf parsley, stemmed and minced

½   cup grated parmigiano-reggiano

1 Heat the stock in a 2-qt. saucepan over medium heat until it begins to simmer; keep warm. Meanwhile, melt 2 tbsp. butter in a 6-qt. saucepan over medium heat. Add the pancetta and onions, and cook, stirring, until the onions are golden, about 10 minutes. Add the oil and increase the heat to high; add the rice and stir to coat well.

2 Add about ¾ cup warm stock and cook, stirring constantly, until most of the stock has been absorbed. Add about ¾ cup more stock. Continue cooking, stirring and adding stock as needed (you should use about 5 cups of stock total), until the rice is tender but firm to the bite, about 20 minutes.

3 Remove from the heat and season to taste with salt and pepper. Stir in the remaining stock and butter along with the peas, parsley, and ¼ cup parmigiano. Cover and allow to rest for a few minutes.

4 Divide the risotto among 4 bowls. Serve with additional parmigiano.

Wine Pairing *The vegetal and buttery flavors of this dish make it a good match for a medium-bodied soave from the Veneto.*

Artichokes, a quintessential ingredient in antipasti, for sale at a market in Rome.

BREAD AND TOMATO SALAD

Panzanella

SERVES 10

This classic salad—a quick toss of toasted day-old bread with good olive oil, ripe tomatoes, fresh herbs, and other brightly flavored ingredients—epitomizes the ingenuity and ease of Italian cooking.

1   1-lb. loaf country-style white bread (pictured below), cut into 1½-inch-thick slices

½   cup olive oil, plus more for brushing

1   pint cherry tomatoes

1   red bell pepper

    Kosher salt and freshly ground black pepper, to taste

2   cups packed baby arugula

½   cup oil-cured black olives, seeded

¼   cup roughly chopped parsley

½   small red onion, thinly sliced

½   small cucumber, thinly sliced

¼   cup red wine vinegar

1   clove garlic, minced

    Zest and juice of 1 lemon

1 Build a medium-hot fire in a charcoal grill or heat a gas grill to medium-high. (Alternatively, arrange an oven rack 4 inches from the broiler element and heat broiler to high.) Brush the bread slices with oil and toss the tomatoes and bell pepper with 2 tbsp. oil; season all of the ingredients with salt and pepper. Place the bread and vegetables on the grill and cook, turning as needed, until the bread is toasted and the tomatoes begin to burst, about 5 minutes. Remove the bread and tomatoes, and continue cooking the bell pepper until it is charred all over, about 7 minutes more. Let the pepper cool, and then peel and remove the seeds; thinly slice and transfer to a large bowl along with the tomatoes, arugula, olives, parsley, onion, and cucumber. Cut the bread slices into 1½-inch cubes and add to the salad

2 To serve, whisk together the remaining oil, vinegar, garlic, lemon juice, and zest in a small bowl; pour over the salad, toss to combine, and season with salt and pepper.

Cooking Note *A refreshing way to start a meal, this salad becomes a more substantial dish when topped with grilled chicken or steak, which allows the bread to soak up the meat's flavorful juices.*

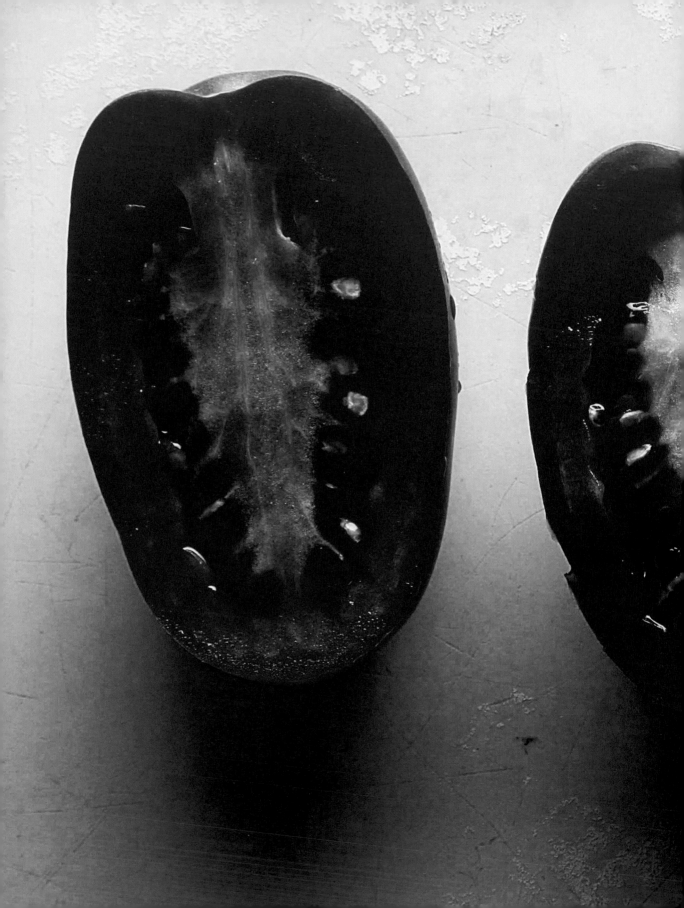

Soups

*Italian soups are soulful simmers, like
flavorful summer vegetable, rustic meatball-
studded escarole, or the kind of hearty
minestrone you crave on a winter's day.*

VEGETABLE SOUP

Zuppa di Verdure

SERVES 12

Chef and cookbook author Lidia Bastianich provided the recipe for this delicious soup, in which the vegetables are cooked quickly to preserve their bright flavor.

½   cup packed basil leaves

¼   cup extra-virgin olive oil, plus more for drizzling

2   tbsp. minced flat-leaf parsley

4   cloves garlic

½   medium onion, cut into chunks

8   oz. red new potatoes, cut into ½-inch cubes

3   stalks celery, minced

2   medium carrots, minced

2   plum tomatoes, cored and minced

    Kosher salt, to taste

3   oz. spinach, trimmed and rinsed (about 2 loosely packed cups)

1½   cups canned cannellini beans, rinsed

1   cup fresh or frozen green peas

½   small head frisée, leaves cut into bite-size pieces (about 2 cups)

    Freshly ground black pepper, to taste

    Freshly grated parmigiano-reggiano, for serving

1 Place half the basil, 2 tbsp. oil, parsley, garlic, and onion in the bowl of a food processor and process until slightly chunky. Heat the remaining oil in an 8-qt. pot over medium-high heat and add the herb-garlic mixture. Cook, stirring often, until the juices from the onion mixture have evaporated, about 5 minutes. Add the potatoes, celery, carrots, and tomatoes. Cook, stirring often, until the vegetables are golden, about 6 minutes. Add salt and 4 cups water and bring to a boil. Reduce the heat to medium-low; cover and cook, stirring occasionally, until the vegetables are tender, about 20 minutes.

2 Stir in the spinach, beans, peas, and frisée and cook until the greens are wilted and just tender, about 10 minutes; season with salt and pepper and stir in the remaining basil. To serve, ladle the soup into bowls, sprinkle with parmigiano, and drizzle with oil.

Cooking Note *Serve this soup with crusty Italian bread or bruschetta, rubbed with garlic and drizzled with oil.*

BREAD AND TOMATO SOUP

Pappa al Pomodoro
SERVES 6-8

Cooks across Tuscany make this thick, basil-scented tomato soup. The day-old bread softens in the soup, then is whisked to produce the soup's velvety texture. This recipe comes from Coco Lezzone, a 200-year-old trattoria in Florence.

½ cup extra-virgin olive oil

2 cloves garlic, peeled and finely chopped

2 leeks, white and light green parts only, washed and finely chopped

9 cups canned whole peeled tomatoes in juice, puréed

6 cups chicken stock

9 ¾-inch-thick slices day-old Tuscan bread or other country-style white bread (about 1 lb.), halved

2 tbsp. chopped basil leaves

Kosher salt and freshly ground black pepper, to taste

Freshly grated parmigiano-reggiano, for serving

1 Heat ⅓ cup of the oil in a large wide pot over medium heat. Add the garlic and cook until it is light golden, about 2 minutes. Reduce the heat to medium-low, add the leeks, and cook, stirring often, until very soft but not browned, 15–20 minutes. Add the tomatoes and the stock, and stir to combine. Increase the heat to medium-high and bring the soup to a boil. Then reduce the heat to medium-low and simmer, stirring occasionally, for 30 minutes.

2 Remove the pot from the heat. Add the bread, pushing it into the soup with a wooden spoon until each piece is submerged. Add the basil and stir gently to combine. Cover the pot and set it aside to let the bread soak until it is completely softened, about 30 minutes.

3 Uncover the pot and whisk the soup vigorously until the bread breaks down and the soup resembles porridge, 4–5 minutes. Season to taste with salt and pepper. Gently reheat the soup over medium heat. Ladle the soup into warm bowls; drizzle with the remaining olive oil and sprinkle with parmigiano.

Cooking Note *If you don't have day-old bread on hand, dry slices of fresh bread in a 300 degree Fahrenheit oven for about 20 minutes before adding them to the soup.*

MINESTRONE

SERVES 8–10

Minestrone means "big soup," an apt name for this hearty simmer of vegetables, white beans, and pasta in a savory tomato broth. In northwest Italy, minestrone is garnished with pesto, which imparts an herbaceous flavor.

FOR THE PESTO:

2 cups packed basil leaves

½ cup grated parmigiano-reggiano

½ tbsp. extra-virgin olive oil

½ tsp. kosher salt

1 clove garlic, chopped

½ plum tomato, cored

Kosher salt and ground black pepper, to taste

FOR THE SOUP:

¼ cup extra-virgin olive oil

1 oz. pancetta, minced

5 cloves garlic, finely chopped

3 medium carrots, peeled and finely chopped

2 ribs celery, finely chopped

1 yellow onion, finely chopped

½ medium zucchini, chopped

¼ head Savoy cabbage, cored and thinly shredded

8 cups chicken stock

7 drained whole peeled canned tomatoes, chopped

⅓ cup broken dried spaghetti

1 15-oz. can cannellini beans

1 Make the pesto: Process the basil, parmigiano, oil, salt, garlic, and tomato in a food processor until finely ground. Season with salt and pepper, and set aside.

2 Make the soup: Heat the oil in a 6-qt. saucepan over medium-high heat; add the pancetta and cook, stirring often, until the fat has rendered, about 2 minutes. Add the garlic, carrots, celery, and onion and reduce the heat to medium; cook, covered and stirring occasionally, until crisp-tender, 12–15 minutes. Add the zucchini and cabbage; cook, covered, until wilted, 3–5 minutes. Add the stock and tomatoes, and bring to a boil. Add the pasta and cook until al dente, about 8 minutes. Mash half the beans with a fork; add to the soup along with the whole beans—cook until warmed through. Season with salt and pepper. Ladle the soup into bowls; serve with pesto dolloped on top.

Cooking Note *You can save time by using store-bought basil pesto rather than making it from scratch, and the finished soup will still be delicious.*

ESCAROLE SOUP

SERVES 8–10

This recipe for rustic escarole soup comes from SAVEUR's executive editor Dana Bowen. The bitter green reveals its sweet and earthy aspects as meatballs enriched with cheese simmer to succulence.

1   lb. ground beef

½   cup seasoned bread crumbs

½   cup grated parmigiano-reggiano, plus more for serving

½   cup grated pecorino romano

½   cup olive oil

1   tbsp. dried Italian seasoning

3   cloves garlic, thinly sliced, plus 1 minced

2   medium yellow onions, thinly sliced, plus 1 minced

1   small bunch flat-leaf parsley, minced

1   egg, lightly beaten

Kosher salt and freshly ground black pepper, to taste

2   large heads escarole, cored, cut into 2-inch pieces

8   cups chicken stock

Cooked white rice, for serving

1 Mix the beef, bread crumbs, parmigiano, pecorino, ¼ cup oil, Italian seasoning, minced garlic and onion, parsley, egg, salt, and pepper in a bowl. Form into thirty 1½-inch meatballs, chill.

2 Heat the remaining oil in an 8-qt. saucepan over medium-high heat. Add the sliced garlic and onions; cook until lightly browned, about 10 minutes. Add the escarole; cook until wilted, about 6 minutes. Add the stock; bring to a boil. Reduce the heat to medium-low. Add the meatballs; cook until the meatballs are cooked through, about 20 minutes. Season with salt and pepper. Serve over rice, and top with more parmigiano and black pepper.

Cooking Note *The generously seasoned meatballs in this soup can be made with ground chicken or turkey in place of the beef called for here.*

Pasta

*The Italian way with noodles is legendary.
Pasta is a canvas for creativity, whether
mixed with a rich ragù, a vibrant vegetable
sauté, or a velvety sauce of cheese and cream.*

TAGLIATELLE WITH BOLOGNESE SAUCE

Tagliatelle con Ragù alla Bolognese

SERVES 4

Cooks in the city of Bologna and surrounding hills of Emilia-Romagna take pride in their signature slow-simmered meat sauce tossed with fresh egg pasta. This recipe comes from chef Anna Nanni, at Trattoria Amerigo dal 1934, a beloved restaurant in the region.

1	28-oz. can whole peeled tomatoes in juice
¼	cup extra-virgin olive oil
2	tbsp. unsalted butter
1	rib celery, finely chopped
½	medium yellow onion, finely chopped
½	medium carrot, finely chopped
	Kosher salt and freshly ground black pepper, to taste
1¼	lbs. ground beef chuck
½	lb. ground pork shoulder
1	4-oz. piece pancetta, finely chopped
½	cup dry red wine
2	tbsp. tomato paste
1	lb. fresh egg pasta, such as tagliatelle
	Grated parmigiano-reggiano, for serving

1 Put the tomatoes and their juice into a blender; purée until smooth and set aside.

2 Heat the oil and butter in a large heavy-bottomed pot over medium heat. Add the celery, onion, and carrot, season with salt and pepper, and cook, stirring frequently, until soft and lightly browned, about 15 minutes. Reduce the heat to low and cook, stirring occasionally, until very soft and caramelized, about 15 minutes more.

3 Add the beef and pork and cook, stirring and breaking up the meat with a wooden spoon, until the meat begins to brown, about 10 minutes. Add the pancetta and continue cooking, stirring occasionally, until its fat has rendered, about 10 minutes more. Increase the heat to medium, add the wine, and simmer, stirring constantly, until evaporated, about 5 minutes. Add the tomato paste and cook, stirring frequently, for 2 minutes. Add the reserved tomato purée, reduce the heat to low, and simmer, stirring occasionally, until the sauce is very thick, about 3 hours. Season the ragù with salt and pepper.

4 Bring a large pot of salted water to a boil, and add the pasta; cook until al dente, about 7 minutes. Drain the pasta and add it to the ragù; toss until the pasta is well coated with sauce. Serve with grated parmigiano.

Wine Pairing *An earthy, rustic red, such as a sagrantino from Umbria, stands up well to the sweet-savory flavor of this meaty sauce.*

SPAGHETTI CARBONARA

SERVES 4

This sumptuous pasta dish is easy to prepare: Simply toss hot spaghetti with the rest of the ingredients, and a velvety sauce comes together in seconds.

4	tbsp. extra-virgin olive oil
4	oz. thinly sliced guanciale or pancetta cut into ½-inch pieces
2	tsp. freshly cracked black pepper, plus more to taste
1¾	cups finely grated parmigiano-reggiano
1	egg plus 3 yolks
	Kosher salt, to taste
1	lb. spaghetti

1 Heat the oil in a 10-inch skillet over medium heat. Add the guanciale and cook, stirring occasionally, until it is lightly browned, 6–8 minutes. Add the pepper and cook, stirring occasionally, until fragrant, 2 minutes more. Transfer the guanciale mixture to a large bowl and let it cool slightly; add 1½ cups parmigiano and the egg and yolks and stir to combine; set aside.

2 Meanwhile, bring a 6-qt. pot of salted water to a boil. Add the pasta; cook until al dente, 8–10 minutes. Reserve ¾ cup water; drain the pasta and transfer it to the guanciale mixture. Toss, adding the pasta water a little at a time to make a creamy sauce. Season with salt and pepper; serve with the remaining parmigiano.

Wine Pairing *This creamy pasta pairs well with a pinot bianco, which has just enough green-apple tartness to cut through the richness of the sauce.*

SPAGHETTI AND MEATBALLS

SERVES 8

Lou Di Palo, owner of Di Palo Fine Foods in New York City's Little Italy, shared his grandmother's recipe for these delicious, ricotta-rich meatballs.

¼ cup olive oil

5 cloves garlic, finely chopped

1 tbsp. dried parsley

1 tbsp. dried basil

2 28-oz. cans whole peeled tomatoes in juice, crushed

Kosher salt and freshly ground black pepper, to taste

¼ cup sugar

10 oz. ground pork

5 oz. ground beef chuck

5 oz. ground veal

⅓ cup shredded provolone

⅓ cup whole-milk ricotta

¼ cup finely grated parmigiano-reggiano

¼ cup finely grated pecorino romano, plus more for serving

¾ cup bread crumbs

3 eggs, lightly beaten

1 lb. spaghetti, cooked

2 tbsp. finely chopped flat-leaf parsley, for serving

1 To make the sauce, heat 2 tbsp. oil and 3 cloves garlic in a 6-qt. saucepan over medium heat; cook until lightly browned, about 3 minutes. Add the dried parsley, basil, tomatoes, salt, and pepper; cook for 60 minutes. Add the sugar; cook until the sauce is reduced and thick, about 20 minutes.

2 To make the meatballs, mix the remaining garlic, pork, chuck, veal, provolone, ricotta, parmigiano, pecorino, bread crumbs, eggs, salt, and pepper in a bowl, and form into eight 2½-inch meatballs, about 6 oz. each.

3 Heat the remaining oil in a 12-inch skillet over medium-high heat. Working in batches, add the meatballs; cook, turning, until browned, about 10 minutes. Transfer to the sauce; cook until cooked through, about 30 minutes. Serve the meatballs and sauce over spaghetti, and sprinkle with parsley.

Wine Pairing *A big plate of spaghetti and meatballs goes well with a spicy, fruity red, like a southern Italian primitivo or an Umbrian sagrantino.*

A counterman in mid-service at Di Palo's, an Italian specialty store in Manhattan's Little Italy.

SWEAT IT OUT

Many Italian sauces, soups, and risottos start the same way: by gently sautéing aromatic ingredients in olive oil to create a base known as *soffritto,* whose flavors will carry throughout the dish. To start, cook minced aromatics—onions, garlic, carrots, and sometimes celery, parsley, pancetta or bacon, and even chile flakes—in a few tablespoons of olive oil until the vegetables' sugars begin to caramelize, but not burn: The heat should be as low as possible; the longer the cooking, the deeper and richer the flavor will be. How long a *soffritto* should cook and when the rest of the dish's components should be added depends on what you're making:

As a rule you want as much caramelization as possible for luxurious ragùs (such as the tagliatelle with bolognese sauce on page 44) and stews, and a more lightly cooked *soffritto* for lighter vegetable soups (like the summery vegetable soup on page 34) and risottos. Either way, many Italian home cooks credit successful dishes to a well-made *soffritto*.

IN PRAISE OF PORK

Full of flavor, rich, and subtly sweet, cured pork jowl, known as *guanciale* (pictured below), is one of our favorite Italian ingredients. When sliced into batons and browned, the tender, flavorful meat and rendered fat add savory depth to Italy's most beloved pasta dishes, such as spaghetti carbonara (see page 47 for a recipe). The beauty of *guanciale*, apart from its generous dose of concentrated flavor and fat, is its versatility: The pork can simply be sliced and sautéed with vegetables, added to stewed fava beans, baked into a frittata, simmered in soups and tomato sauces, or cooked with meat or fish so that its fragrant fat suffuses the dish, adding maximum flavor with minimal effort. Usually sold in shrink-wrapped pieces or sliced, *guanciale* is less salty but fattier and more flavorful than its meaty cousin, pancetta—Italian salt-cured pork belly—and its texture is somewhat softer. Even if you can't easily find *guanciale* at your local market, most cured Italian meats, including pancetta, prosciutto, and speck (smoked, dry-cured ham), or American-style bacon (look for thick-sliced, applewood-smoked varieties) can be used to infuse sauces and dishes with the subtly porky flavor that makes Italian home cooking so good.

CAVATELLI WITH BROCCOLI RABE AND SAUSAGE

SERVES 2

Broccoli rabe, also known as broccolini and rapini, reveals its sweet side when it is cooked until just tender. Fennel-scented Italian sausage is a natural match.

Kosher salt, to taste

1 lb. broccoli rabe (pictured below), roughly chopped

⅓ cup extra-virgin olive oil

4 oz. sweet Italian sausage, casings removed

¾ tsp. crushed red chile flakes

6 cloves garlic, crushed

12 oz. cavatelli or penne pasta

4 oz. grated parmigiano-reggiano

1 Bring a large pot of salted water to a boil and add the broccoli rabe; boil until crisp-tender, 4 minutes. Drain and set aside.

2 Heat the oil in a 12-inch skillet and add the sausage; cook, breaking it into chunks with a wooden spoon, until browned, 6–8 minutes. Add the chile flakes and garlic and cook until fragrant, 3–4 minutes more.

3 Bring a large pot of salted water to a boil and add the pasta; cook until al dente, 7–8 minutes. Drain, reserving about 1 cup of the pasta water, and add the pasta to the sausage along with the broccoli rabe and ¾ of the parmigiano; toss together until well combined, adding a few tablespoons of pasta water to create a sauce, if necessary. Sprinkle the remaining parmigiano over the top before serving.

Wine Pairing *Fresh, bright whites like pinot bianco and pinot grigio from Trentino pair well with the sweet and bitter flavors in this dish.*

TRENETTE WITH PESTO, GREEN BEANS, AND POTATOES

SERVES 4

Ligurians know how to make the most of their vegetable harvest, as in this regional classic combining thin green beans, new potatoes, pesto, and trenette, Liguria's local take on linguine.

3   cups packed basil

½   cup extra-virgin olive oil

3   tbsp. finely grated parmigiano-reggiano

2   tbsp. finely grated pecorino romano

2   tbsp. pine nuts (pictured below)

1   clove garlic, finely chopped

Kosher salt and freshly ground black pepper, to taste

1   lb. trenette or linguine pasta

Kosher salt, to taste

8   oz. haricots verts, trimmed

8   oz. baby red potatoes, roasted until fork tender, and halved

Finely chopped flat-leaf parsley, to garnish

1 Make the pesto: Process the basil, oil, cheeses, nuts, and garlic in a food processor until smooth. Season with salt and pepper; set aside.

2 Bring a 6-qt. saucepan of salted water to a boil over high heat; add the pasta and cook, stirring, until half-cooked, about 5 minutes. Add the haricots verts, and cook, stirring, until the pasta is al dente and the vegetables are tender, about 3 minutes more. Drain the pasta and vegetables, reserving ¼ cup cooking water, and transfer to a large bowl along with the potatoes and pesto; toss to combine, adding a couple of tablespoons of reserved cooking water, if needed, to make a smooth sauce. Garnish with parsley.

Wine Pairing *The Piedmont's crisp arneis makes a refreshing match for this light and simple pasta dish.*

PASTA WITH TOMATOES AND EGGPLANT

Pasta alla Norma

SERVES 4–6

Ricotta salata, a firm and piquant sheep's milk cheese, is the finishing touch to the silky tomato and eggplant sauce on this full-flavored pasta dish.

2	medium eggplants, cut into ¾-inch cubes
7	tbsp. extra-virgin olive oil
	Kosher salt and freshly ground black pepper, to taste
1	small yellow onion, minced
1	tsp. crushed red chile flakes
5	cloves garlic, minced
1	28-oz. can whole peeled tomatoes in juice, crushed
16	fresh basil leaves, torn into small pieces by hand
1	lb. bucatini or spaghetti
4	oz. ricotta salata, grated

1 Heat the oven to 500°F. Put the eggplant into a bowl and drizzle with 4 tbsp. oil. Toss to combine and season with salt and pepper. Transfer the eggplant to 2 baking sheets and bake, turning occasionally, until soft and caramelized, about 20 minutes. Transfer to a rack and set aside.

2 Heat remaining oil in a 5-qt. pot over medium heat. Add the onions and cook, stirring, until soft, about 10 minutes. Add the chile flakes and garlic and cook, stirring, until the garlic softens, about 3 minutes. Add the tomatoes and half of the basil, season with salt, and cook until heated through, about 5 minutes.

3 Meanwhile, bring a large pot of salted water to a boil. Add the pasta and cook, stirring occasionally, until just al dente, about 9 minutes. Drain the pasta and transfer to the tomato sauce. Stir in the reserved eggplant and toss to combine. Stir in the remaining basil and season with salt. To serve, transfer the pasta to a platter and garnish with ricotta salata.

Wine Pairing *A young chianti, or a medium-bodied lacrima di Morro d'Alba from Le Marche, will allow the flavors of the vegetables in this dish to shine through.*

Anna Dente, the owner and chef of Osteria di San Cesario in Rome, plates her rigatoni.

CORKSCREW PASTA WITH ALMOND PESTO

Busiate alla Trapanese

SERVES 6–8

In this rich pesto—a specialty of the seaside city of Trapani, Sicily—tangy tomatoes, meaty almonds, and sweet golden raisins play off of briny capers and anchovies.

1	pint cherry tomatoes
¾	cup sliced almonds, toasted
½	cup packed basil
½	cup finely grated parmigiano-reggiano, plus more for serving
5	tbsp. extra-virgin olive oil
2	tbsp. golden raisins
2	tbsp. capers, drained
¼	tsp. crushed red chile flakes
3	anchovy fillets in oil, drained
2	cloves garlic, chopped
1	pepperoncini, stemmed, seeded, and roughly chopped
	Kosher salt and freshly ground black pepper, to taste
1	lb. busiate or fusilli

1 Make the pesto: Place the tomatoes in a food processor and process until finely chopped, then pour the tomatoes into a fine strainer and drain off excess juices. Process the tomatoes along with the almonds, basil, parmigiano, oil, raisins, capers, chile flakes, anchovies, garlic, and pepperoncini in a food processor until finely ground. Season with salt and pepper, and refrigerate until needed.

2 Bring a large pot of salted water to a boil over high heat; working in batches, add the pasta and cook, stirring, until al dente, about 8 minutes. Drain, reserving ¼ cup cooking water, and transfer the pasta to a large bowl along with the pesto; toss to combine, adding a couple of spoonfuls of cooking water, if needed, to create a smooth sauce. Transfer to a large serving platter or bowls and serve with more parmigiano.

Cooking Note *In place of the cherry tomatoes called for here, you could substitute two medium-size tomatoes or two cups of canned whole peeled tomatoes in their juices.*

LINGUINE WITH CLAMS AND CHILES

SERVES 4

As fresh clams cook, they release a sweet liquor that makes a voluptuous sauce when it mingles with white wine and olive oil. Be sure to undercook the pasta slightly so it can finish cooking in the sauce and absorb its rich flavor.

Kosher salt, to taste

1 lb. pasta, preferably linguine

⅓ cup extra-virgin olive oil, plus more for drizzling

4 oz. pancetta, minced

2 cloves garlic, thinly sliced crosswise

1 Fresno or holland chile, stemmed and thinly sliced crosswise

2¾ lbs. littleneck clams (about 30; pictured below), scrubbed clean

⅓ cup dry white wine

3 tbsp. roughly chopped fresh flat-leaf parsley

1 Bring a large pot of salted water to a boil. Add the pasta and cook, stirring occasionally, until just al dente, about 6 minutes. Drain the pasta, reserving ½ cup pasta water, and set aside. Meanwhile, heat the oil in a 12-inch skillet over medium heat. Add the pancetta and cook, stirring occasionally, until just crisp, about 5 minutes. Using a slotted spoon, transfer the pancetta to a paper towel, and set aside.

2 Return the skillet to medium heat and add the garlic and half the chiles; cook, stirring often, until the garlic is golden brown, about 3 minutes. Add the clams and wine, increase the heat to high, and cook, covered, swirling the pan occasionally, until the clams open and release their juices, 5–10 minutes. Using tongs, transfer the clams to a plate; set aside. Bring the sauce to a boil over high heat, return the pancetta to the pan, and add the reserved pasta and ¼ cup cooking liquid. Cook, tossing the pasta occasionally, until the sauce clings to the pasta, about 2 minutes. Sprinkle in some more of the pasta cooking water if the pasta seems dry. Add 2 tbsp. parsley, season with salt, and toss to combine. Transfer the pasta to a serving bowl, arrange the clams over the pasta, and pour any clam juices from the plate over the pasta. Drizzle the pasta with more olive oil and garnish with the remaining chiles and parsley.

Wine Pairing *A light, crisp white, such as a soave classico from the Veneto or a young Le Marchian verdicchio, pairs beautifully with the saline flavors in this dish.*

PASTA WITH CHICKEN

Pappardelle al Pollo

SERVES 4

Cooks across Italy toss ribbons of fresh pasta with luscious braises of wild boar, rabbit, and other game meats. We've found that the rich, dark thigh meat of chicken makes a fine substitute for game in this classic ragù.

1	tbsp. extra-virgin olive oil
1	¼-lb. slab pancetta, cut into ½-inch cubes
4	bone-in chicken thighs (about 1¼ lbs.)
	Kosher salt and freshly ground black pepper, to taste
4	cloves garlic, thinly sliced
2	dried mushrooms, such as porcini, finely chopped (about ⅛ oz.)
1	small carrot, finely chopped
1	tbsp. tomato paste
¼	cup white wine vinegar
3	cups chicken broth
1	pint grape or cherry tomatoes (about 10 oz.)
4	tbsp. chopped tarragon leaves
1	lb. dried or fresh pappardelle or dried fettuccine
¾	cup grated parmigiano-reggiano

1 Heat oil in a Dutch oven over medium-high heat. Add the pancetta and cook, stirring occasionally, until brown and crisp, about 10 minutes. Using a slotted spoon, transfer the pancetta to a plate and set aside. Return pot to heat and increase heat to medium-high. Season chicken with salt and pepper and add to pot; cook, flipping once, until browned, about 10 minutes. Transfer chicken to a plate and set aside.

2 Pour off all but 1 tbsp. fat. Return pot to heat and add garlic, mushrooms, and carrot and cook, stirring frequently, until soft, about 8 minutes. Add tomato paste and cook, stirring frequently, until lightly browned, about 3 minutes. Add vinegar and cook, stirring frequently, until almost evaporated, about 1 minute. Return pancetta and chicken to pot, along with broth, tomatoes, and 2 tbsp. tarragon. Bring broth to a boil; reduce heat to medium-low. Simmer until chicken is tender and broth has reduced by half, about 40 minutes. Transfer chicken to a plate, allow to cool, and remove and discard skin and bones. Tear chicken into chunks and return to pot; season sauce with salt and pepper and set aside.

3 Meanwhile, bring a pot of salted water to a boil. Add pasta and cook until just short of al dente, about 7 minutes. Reserve 1 cup pasta water. Drain pasta and transfer to pot containing chicken sauce; set over high heat. Bring to a boil, stir in ½ cup parmigiano, and cook, tossing occasionally with tongs, until sauce thickens and clings to pasta, about 2 minutes. (If sauce is too dry, pour in a little pasta water.) Add remaining tarragon and season with salt and pepper. Transfer pasta to 4 bowls and sprinkle with remaining parmigiano.

Main Dishes

The pinnacle of Italian menus are elemental foods—pork chops, steak, lamb, fish—served with flavorful, herb-flecked sauces and peak of season vegetables.

SWEET AND SOUR GLAZED PORK CHOPS

Maiale in Agrodolce

SERVES 4

The tantalizing balance of sweet and sour is a recurring theme throughout Italian regional cuisines. Here, honey and balsamic vinegar create an intensely flavorful glaze for grilled pork chops; roasted potatoes would make a perfect side.

4	10-oz. bone-in pork chops, frenched
3	tbsp. extra-virgin olive oil
	Kosher salt and freshly ground black pepper, to taste
⅓	cup balsamic vinegar
2	tbsp. honey
4	tbsp. unsalted butter
1	sprig fresh rosemary, torn into 1-inch pieces

1 Put the pork chops on a plate; drizzle with the oil; season generously with salt and pepper. Let sit for 30 minutes.

2 Meanwhile, build a medium-hot fire in a charcoal grill or heat a gas grill to medium-high heat. (Alternatively, heat a stove-top grill pan over medium-high heat.) Combine the vinegar and honey in a 1-qt. saucepan and cook over medium heat until reduced to about ¼ cup. Stir in the butter and rosemary and set aside.

3 Put the pork chops on the grill and cook, occasionally turning and basting with the balsamic mixture, until browned and cooked through, 12–14 minutes. Transfer to a platter and let sit for 5 minutes before serving.

Wine Pairing *This sweet-tart dish calls for a sassy, light red, like Trentino's teroldego rotiliano or barolo's softer cousin, barbaresco, from the Piedmont in northwest Italy. An interesting white, Friuli's amphora-aged vitovska, has cidery notes to complement the pork's flavors.*

SWORDFISH PUTTANESCA

SERVES 4

Swordfish has luxuriously meaty flesh that's as well suited as any fish we know to the bracing sauce of tomatoes, capers, chiles, and garlic known as *puttanesca*. Serve it with pasta simply dressed with olive oil and parmigiano-reggiano.

4   swordfish steaks (about 6 oz. each and ⅜ inch thick), skin removed

    Kosher salt and freshly ground black pepper, to taste

¼   cup extra-virgin olive oil

2   cloves garlic, thinly sliced

2   anchovies in oil, finely chopped

2   cups whole peeled canned tomatoes, drained and minced

½   cup large green olives, such as Cerignola, pitted and roughly chopped

3   tbsp. salt-packed capers, soaked and drained

¼   tsp. crushed red chile flakes

2   tbsp. roughly chopped flat-leaf parsley

1   tbsp. fresh lemon juice

1 Season the swordfish with salt and pepper. Heat the oil in a 12-inch skillet over high heat. Working in two batches, add the swordfish and cook, flipping once, until golden brown and medium-rare, about 3 minutes total. Transfer the swordfish to a plate, leaving oil in the skillet.

2 Reduce the heat to medium; add the garlic and anchovies and cook, stirring, until soft, about 3 minutes. Add the tomatoes, olives, capers, and chile flakes and cook, stirring, until fragrant, about 5 minutes. Return the swordfish steaks to the skillet, nestling them in the sauce, and add the parsley and lemon juice; cook until the fish is cooked to desired doneness. To serve, transfer the swordfish to a platter and spoon sauce over the top.

Fishmongers display the catch of the day at a market in Catania, Sicily.

THE BLUES

Italians have a great love of dark-fleshed, meaty fish, such as the swordfish called for in the recipe on page 72; their oily flesh stands up to emphatically flavored ingredients, like those used in a classic olive- and caper-spiked *puttanesca* sauce or in a garlicky reduction of red wine. But swordfish, often referred to as the steak of fish, is just one character in a large cast of what's known in Italy as *pesce azzurro*, or blue fish (so named for their silvery-blue skin, as compared to paler-skinned varieties, which tend to have a more demure flavor). Tuna is another popular *pesce azzurro*, particularly among Sicilian cooks, but smaller eel, bluefish ❶, mackerel ❷, sardines ❸, and anchovies take just as well to strong seasonings, from bacon to hot peppers, that would overwhelm milder fish. Thanks to their high oil content (full of healthy omega-3 fatty acids), these fish also remain moist and delicious when grilled, fried, or smoked. The best thing about these smaller *pesce azzurro*, aside from their fine flavor and versatility? Their affordability and abundance.

€7.00 VNA

€7.

filetti di Acciughe
sott'olio
2,00

filetti di Acciughe
sott'olio
€3,00
uno

filetti di Acciughe
sott'olio
€7,00
uno

filetti
di acciu
2,50
uno

Salt-cured sardines, oil-packed
anchovies, and other preserved fish
for sale at a market in Sicily.

HERRING FIRST QUALITY
ARINGHE PRIMA QUALITA

ROASTED LAMB SHOULDER
WITH POTATOES

Cosciotto di Agnello con Patate

SERVES 8

Roasted herb-crusted lamb is a traditional Easter dish across Sicily. In this version, potatoes cooked right alongside the lamb drink in the savory pan drippings.

¾   cup extra-virgin olive oil

2   tbsp. crushed red chile flakes

2   tbsp. dried oregano

4   cloves garlic, minced

1   bunch parsley, minced

    Kosher salt and freshly ground black pepper, to taste

1   6–7-lb. leg of lamb, trimmed

8   large russet potatoes, peeled and quartered

1 Heat the oven to 500°F. In a medium bowl, combine the oil, chile flakes, oregano, garlic, parsley, and salt and pepper to make a paste, and rub the paste over the surface of the lamb. Set the lamb in a large roasting pan and place the pan in the oven; roast until the lamb is browned, about 30 minutes.

2 Reduce the oven temperature to 400°F, cover the lamb with aluminum foil, and continue cooking for 40 minutes.

3 Remove the foil, add the potatoes to the pan, and toss with the rendered fat; continue cooking until the potatoes are tender and an instant-read thermometer inserted into the thickest part of the lamb reads 140°F, about 45–50 minutes more. Let rest for 20 minutes before serving.

Wine Pairing *Sicily's rosso di Etna has the mineral backbone to enhance the sweet, herbaceous flavors of this roasted lamb.*

BRAISED VEAL SHANKS

Osso Buco

SERVES 6

Rick Moonen, chef at RM Seafood in Las Vegas, gave us his mother's recipe for these falling-off-the-bone veal shanks. A *gremolata* of chopped parsley, garlic, and lemon zest gives the dish a vibrant boost; add a side of mashed potatoes to soak up the rich gravy.

6	1½-inch-thick cross-cut veal shanks, tied with kitchen twine
	Kosher salt and freshly ground black pepper, to taste
1	cup flour
2	tbsp. canola oil
3	tbsp. unsalted butter
2	large onions, minced
2	medium carrots, minced
2	ribs celery, minced
2	tbsp. tomato paste
1	bunch flat-leaf parsley
5	sprigs fresh thyme
2	bay leaves
1	750-ml bottle dry white wine
1	cup veal stock (optional)
8	cloves garlic, minced
	Zest of 3 lemons

1 Heat the oven to 325°F. Season veal shanks with salt and pepper. Put flour on a plate and dredge veal in flour, shaking off excess; transfer to a plate. Heat oil in a 6-qt. Dutch oven over medium-high heat. Working in 2 batches, add veal shanks and cook, flipping once, until browned, about 10 minutes. Transfer veal shanks to a plate. Add butter to pot; stir in onions, carrots, and celery and cook, stirring and scraping any browned bits from bottom of pot with a wooden spoon, until soft, about 10 minutes. Stir in tomato paste and cook for 2 minutes. Tie 3 parsley sprigs and thyme with kitchen twine and add to pot along with bay leaves, veal shanks, wine, and veal stock or 1 cup water. Bring to a simmer, season lightly with salt and pepper, and cover.

2 Transfer pot to oven and cook until veal is nearly falling off the bone, about 1½ hours. Transfer veal shanks to a plate and cover with aluminum foil. Discard herb bundle and bay leaves. Heat pot over medium heat and reduce liquid by half. Transfer veal shanks back to pot, spoon over liquid, and cover to keep warm. Meanwhile, finely chop the remaining parsley leaves and toss in a bowl with the garlic and lemon zest. Sprinkle some of parsley mixture over veal shanks and serve family style from the pot along with the remaining parsley mixture.

Wine Pairing *These succulent shanks call for a medium-bodied red; try a lacrima di Morro d'Alba from Le Marche, or a young, fruitier barolo.*

STEAK WITH HERB SAUCE

Bistecca con Salsa delle Erbe

SERVES 2

A well-marbled cut of beef prepared Tuscan-style—simply rubbed with salt, pepper, and olive oil and grilled—produces a succulent and flavorful steak. Serve it with roasted potatoes and sautéed greens.

1 cup packed basil leaves (pictured below)

1 cup packed flat-leaf parsley leaves

2 tbsp. packed fresh oregano leaves

1 tbsp. packed fresh rosemary leaves

1 tbsp. packed fresh thyme leaves

1 tbsp. packed fresh tarragon leaves

2 cloves garlic, minced

¾ cup plus 2 tbsp. extra-virgin olive oil

Kosher salt and freshly ground black pepper, to taste

1 24-oz. 2–3-inch-thick rib-eye, strip, or porterhouse steak

1 Put the herbs and garlic on a cutting board and finely chop together with a large knife. Transfer the herb mixture to a small bowl and stir in ¾ cup oil. Season the herb sauce with salt and pepper, cover with plastic wrap, and set aside for at least 1 hour to let the flavors meld. Meanwhile, put the steak on a plate, season generously with salt and pepper, and rub with 2 tbsp. oil.

2 Build a medium-hot fire in a charcoal grill or heat a gas grill to medium-high. (Alternatively, heat an oiled grill pan over medium-high heat.) Cook the steak, flipping once, until it is browned and cooked to desired doneness, 8–10 minutes for medium rare. Transfer the steak to a platter and let it rest for 5 minutes. Slice the steak against the grain and spoon some reserved sauce over the top.

Wine Pairing *Nothing goes better with this juicy grilled steak and its herbaceous garnish than Tuscany's muscular chianti classico.*

PULLED PORK ITALIANO SANDWICH

SERVES 8

The Philadelphia sandwich shop DiNic's serves this mouthwatering sandwich of wine-and-herb-braised pork, provolone cheese, and delectably bitter broccoli rabe. Rather than making a sandwich, you can serve the pork on its own.

3	tbsp. ground fennel seeds
3	tbsp. dried parsley
1½	tbsp. dried thyme
3½	tsp. crushed red chile flakes
1	6–7-lb. pork shoulder, butterflied
3	sprigs rosemary, stemmed and finely chopped
1	head garlic, minced
	Kosher salt and freshly ground black pepper, to taste
4	cups beef stock
½	cup red wine
1	medium yellow onion, thinly sliced
1	bay leaf
½	cup crushed canned whole peeled tomatoes
2	lbs. broccoli rabe
¼	cup canola oil
32	slices sharp provolone
8	12-inch crusty Italian rolls
16	roasted Italian hot peppers (optional; pictured below)

1 Heat the oven to 450°F. Combine fennel, parsley, thyme, and 3 tsp. chile flakes in a small bowl; set aside. Open pork shoulder on a work surface, and spread with half of fennel mixture, rosemary, a quarter of the chopped garlic, salt, and pepper. Roll up shoulder, tie with kitchen twine at 1-inch intervals to secure, and season outside with remaining herb mixture, salt, and pepper. Transfer to a roasting pan, and roast until browned, about 40 minutes. Remove pan from oven, and heat broiler. Add remaining garlic to pan, along with stock, wine, onion, and bay leaf; pour tomatoes over top and sides of pork shoulder. Broil until tomatoes are caramelized, about 20 minutes. Reduce oven temperature to 325°F, cover pork with parchment paper, and cover roasting pan with aluminum foil. Cook until internal temperature of pork reaches 165°F, about 2 hours. Set aside to cool.

2 Transfer pork to a cutting board, and remove bay leaf from pan. Transfer juices to a blender and purée; transfer to a 4-qt. saucepan and keep warm. Pull pork apart into large pieces and add to pan juices.

3 Meanwhile, bring a large pot of salted water to a boil, and add broccoli rabe. Cook, stirring, until just tender, 2–3 minutes. Drain and transfer to a bowl of ice water to cool. Drain, and dry thoroughly with paper towels. Heat oil in a 12-inch skillet. Working in batches if necessary, add remaining chile flakes and the broccoli rabe; cook, stirring, until crisp and warmed through, about 4 minutes. Set aside.

4 Place 4 slices provolone on bottom half of each roll, and cover with pork; top with broccoli rabe, and garnish each sandwich with 2 peppers, if you like.

Servers gather at Trattoria Zero Otto Nove on Arthur Avenue in the Bronx.

EGGPLANT PARMESAN

SERVES 8

This saucy dish is the ultimate Italian-American comfort food. Our recipe calls for lightly frying, but not breading, the eggplant, highlighting the vegetable's earthy flavor and silky texture. Serve with spaghetti and a side of sautéed greens.

3⅓ cups olive oil

½ tsp. crushed red chile flakes

5 cloves garlic, thinly sliced

6 cups canned whole peeled tomatoes in juice, crushed by hand

Kosher salt and ground black pepper, to taste

3 large eggplants (about 3½ lbs.), trimmed and cut lengthwise into ¼-inch-thick slices

8 oz. grated pecorino romano

2 oz. grated parmigiano-reggiano

1 Heat ⅓ cup oil, the chile flakes, and garlic in a 4-qt. saucepan over medium-low heat, and cook, stirring, until the garlic begins to turn golden, about 4 minutes. Add the tomatoes, and cook, stirring occasionally, until the sauce has reduced and thickened, about 3 hours. Season with salt and pepper and set the sauce aside.

2 Meanwhile, heat the remaining oil in a 12-inch high-sided skillet over medium-high heat. Working in batches, add the eggplant slices and fry, turning once, until they are golden brown and pliable, about 2 minutes. Transfer the slices to paper towels to drain and season them with salt and pepper; discard the cooking oil.

3 Heat the oven to 350°F. Spread 1 cup sauce in the bottom of a 9-x-13-inch baking dish, and top with a third of the eggplant slices; top with another cup of sauce, and then sprinkle with a third of the pecorino. Repeat the layering twice more, ending with the pecorino on top; cover the dish with foil. Bake until the eggplant is tender, about 1½ hours. Remove the foil, sprinkle with the parmigiano, and continue baking until the cheese is melted, about 5 minutes.

Wine Pairing *A robust red with rich tannins, such as a chianti or sagrantino, pairs well with the tomato sauce's bright acidity.*

BEPPINO O

BUTT
FROM FRES

Hand made with a "cow er

CELLI®

R CREAM

...g on the surface"®

NET WEIGHT 250g e

Sweets

Berries with freshly whipped custard;
creamy panna cotta; almond-rich meringue
cookies: Italian desserts are simple
pleasures that are blessedly easy to make.

ZABAGLIONE WITH MIXED BERRIES

SERVES 4

A bowlful of berries—whatever is in season and bursting with flavor—makes a lavish dessert with freshly whipped, marsala-spiked custard spooned over the top.

¾   cup sugar

6   egg yolks

½   cup marsala wine

¼   tsp. kosher salt

2   cups heavy cream, chilled

4   cups mixed raspberries, blueberries, blackberries, and hulled, quartered strawberries

    Ground cinnamon, to garnish

1 Whisk together the sugar and yolks in a medium metal bowl until smooth; stir in the marsala and salt. Place the bowl over a saucepan of simmering water, and cook, whisking constantly, until doubled in volume and thickened, about 3 minutes. Remove from the heat and set the zabaglione aside.

2 Meanwhile, put the heavy cream in a bowl, and whisk until stiff peaks form. Add the whipped cream to the zabaglione, and fold gently until evenly combined.

3 Divide the berries among 4 wide, shallow serving bowls and spoon the zabagalione over top. Dust with the cinnamon and serve immediately.

VANILLA PUDDING WITH STRAWBERRIES

Panna Cotta

SERVES 6

Panna cotta translates literally as *cooked cream*, and that's really all it is—a luscious dessert that can be whipped up quickly on the stovetop and left to set in the refrigerator. A syrup of strawberries saturated in a rich wine such as vin santo is the classic companion.

3½ tsp. unflavored powdered gelatin

2⅔ cups heavy cream

¾ cup plus 2 tbsp. sugar

1 vanilla bean, split lengthwise, seeds removed and reserved

2⅔ cups buttermilk

1 lb. strawberries, hulled and halved lengthwise

2 tbsp. vin santo, port, or brandy

1 Put 3 tbsp. cold water into a small bowl and add the gelatin; set aside to let soften for 5 minutes. Meanwhile, heat the cream, ¾ cup sugar, and vanilla bean along with the seeds in a 2-qt. saucepan over medium heat. Cook, stirring often, until the mixture is heated and the sugar dissolves, 5 minutes. Remove the pan from the heat and stir in the soaked gelatin until it's dissolved; add the buttermilk and pour the mixture through a fine strainer into a large measuring cup. Divide the custard between six 8-oz. ramekins and refrigerate until set, about 4 hours.

2 Meanwhile, toss the remaining sugar, strawberries, and vin santo in a medium bowl; refrigerate for 30 minutes. To serve, immerse the ramekins in a baking dish half full of hot water for 5–10 seconds; invert the ramekins onto serving plates to release the panna cotta. Spoon the strawberries and their juice around each panna cotta.

Cooking Note *If fresh berries are not in season, you can substitute fresh pears prepared in the same way.*

Three baristi gather behind the espresso
counter at a Castroni Caffè in Rome.

PINE NUT COOKIES

Pignoli

MAKES ABOUT 3 DOZEN

New York City–based pastry chef and cookbook author Nick Malgieri
taught us the surprisingly simple technique for making these chewy,
pine nut–topped meringue cookies.

2   cups whole blanched
     almonds

½   cup granulated sugar

1   cup confectioners' sugar

3   egg whites, lightly beaten

½   cup pine nuts

1 Heat the oven to 300°F. Combine the almonds and
granulated sugar in a food processor, and process until
very finely ground, about 4 minutes. Add the confectioners'
sugar and egg whites, and process until a smooth dough
forms. Transfer the dough to a piping bag fitted with a
½-inch round tip, and pipe 1-inch mounds, spaced 2 inches
apart, on parchment paper–lined baking sheets. Gently
place 10–12 pine nuts on the top of each mound.

2 Bake the cookies, rotating the baking sheets top to bottom
and front to back halfway through cooking, until golden
brown, about 25 minutes. Let the cookies cool completely
before serving.

Wine Pairing *Vin Santo, the amber-hued Tuscan dessert
wine that's lush with notes of nuts and wood, is the perfect
companion for these rich cookies.*

Cedri, a fragrant citrus fruit, on display in a seaside market on the southern Italian coast.

THE ITALIAN PANTRY

Balsamic Vinegar

This treasured condiment, a specialty of the city of Modena, is made from the juice of local grapes, boiled until sweet and concentrated. That liquid is aged for at least 12 years in small wooden barrels to create aceto balsamico tradizionale, a pricey syrup that's used sparingly to add sweetness to salads and pastas. The vast majority is aged less, though—look for bottles that feature the word condimento or aged. Balsamic vinegar gives agrodolce sauce (see page 71 for a recipe with pork chops) its sweet tang, and is delicious tossed with fresh strawberries.

Bread Crumbs

Since fresh-baked bread is an essential part of every Italian meal, home cooks got into the habit long ago of grating the leftovers and baking them to a crisp, sometimes flavoring the crumbs with herbs, salt, and other seasonings. Bread crumbs are used to bind meatballs and coat foods before frying; they're also sprinkled on top of dishes before roasting or broiling to create a savory crunch. We use our fair share of packaged bread crumbs, but if we have day-old bread, we prefer to make our own, toasting pieces of Italian bread in a 375 degree Fahrenheit oven until they're golden brown and crispy, then crumbling them by hand or milling them in a food processor.

Cannellini Beans

Cannellini beans are white legumes that grow across Umbria and Tuscany; they have firm flesh and an earthy, almost nutty flavor. If you don't have time to soak dry cannellini beans, the canned or jarred precooked versions work just as well in soups, stews, sauces, and as a topping for bruschetta.

THE ITALIAN PANTRY

Continued

Flat-Leaf Parsley

Practically every dish that comes out of the Italian kitchen is showered with a confetti of this herb, which gives a brisk edge to everything it touches. Look for parsley with pert leaves, a bright green color, and snappy stems. The herb stores well wrapped in damp paper towels in a plastic bag in the refrigerator. Chop a bunch and blend it into vegetable soup (see page 34 for a recipe); mash some in a mortar with olive oil, anchovies, lemon juice, and chile flakes to make a salsa verde for grilled meats; toss whole or chopped leaves into a steaming bowl of pasta.

Garlic

Garlic is essential to Italian cooking. Buy a little at a time, so it's as fresh as possible, and seek out the hard-neck variety sold at many farmer's markets— it's distinguished by its fat, juicy cloves arranged around a hard center stem. Harvested in summer and sold throughout the year, hard-neck garlic has a more complex flavor than soft-neck garlic, which is identifiable by its thinner skin, smaller cloves, and more intense flavor. When buying any garlic, look for firm bulbs that have not sprouted, and store them in a cool, dry place.

Grating Cheeses

Parmigiano-reggiano is the king of *grana* cheeses, the hard, aged varieties that Italians cook with, use as a garnish, and savor on their own as an antipasto. Aged for at least 12 months and made from the milk of cows that graze on the plains around the northern Italian city of Parma, this cheese has a sweet, salty, nutty flavor that goes well with tomato-, olive oil–, or butter-based sauces. But it can be pricey; milder, milky grana padano is a good substitute.

Long Pasta

Creamy, cheesy pasta dishes (like spaghetti carbonara; see page 47 for a recipe), and those with copious amounts of smooth sauce (like spaghetti with meatballs; page 48) work best with long pastas. Keep different sizes of dried durum wheat noodles on hand for different purposes: thin spaghettini for lightly flavored sauces; thicker linguine for briny seafood sauces; fettucini for hearty meat sauces. Dried pastas have more heft and bite to them than fresh egg pastas, whose pillowy texture pairs well with butter-based sauces or delicately seasoned, northern Italian–style meat ragùs.

Oil-Cured Anchovy Fillets

These tiny, tender fillets, cured in olive oil, are a secret weapon in the Italian kitchen: Simply mash a couple into a *puttanesca* sauce (see page 72 for a recipe) to create a backbone of flavor, or drizzle the flavorful oil straight from the jar onto steaks and roasted potatoes or into marinades and vinaigrettes. We prefer anchovies in jars, rather than cans, because it's easier to store them once you've opened the jar.

Olives

Brined, cured, or preserved in oil, olives of every variety give an instant boost of salinity to countless Italian classics, whether they're simmered with eggplant in a luscious caponata (see page 13 for a recipe), or tossed into a fresh panzanella salad (page 31). Olives themselves make for an easy, delicious antipasto: Marinate a combination of black and green olives with extra-virgin olive oil, a splash of fresh orange juice, minced orange zest, fresh bay leaves, and black pepper and serve with rustic, crusty bread.

Olive Oil

Italians revere the oil from the fruit of their beloved olive tree: it's used in virtually everything they cook. While it's great to keep bottles from different regions on hand—fruity Ligurian oil is perfect with fish; Tuscan oil has a peppery bite; Sicilian oil tastes of green olives— all you really need in your kitchen is a good, all-purpose extra-virgin olive oil made from the first pressing of olives for sautéing, drizzling into soups, making salad dressings, and even deep-frying. We love California and Spanish oils, as well as Italian.

Red Chile Flakes

Italian cooking isn't known for its overtly spicy foods, but chile heat is often applied to achieve balance in a dish. That's where chile flakes come in handy: to temper slightly bitter sautéed greens, to add dimension to a bruschetta topped with ricotta and olive oil, or to otherwise heighten a dish's flavor. When you're in the mood for a spicy sauce, add chile flakes while making a *soffritto* by sweating garlic, onions, and other ingredients in oil. Purchase chile flakes in small quantities and use within six to eight months for the best flavor and heat.

Risotto Rice

Northern Italy's risottos, such as *risi e bisi* (see page 26 for a recipe), are distinguished by the chubby varieties of rice cultivated in the Po Valley; their starch accounts for the creamy texture of risotto and other rice-based Italian dishes. Medium-grained arborio is the best known, but in recent years, many Italian cooks' rice of choice, *vialone nano,* has become more readily available in American specialty food stores. Its short-grained kernels are more forgiving than arborio's and tend not to overcook as easily.

Short Pasta

Chunky, thick sauces—ones that are studded with ingredients like ground sausage, olives, or chopped vegetables—are best paired with short, sturdy durum wheat pastas, like *penne rigate,* whose ridged, quill-shaped tubes grab hold of the sauce's ingredients. We keep boxes of it on hand, along with the corkscrews known as *fusilli,* and bite-size coin-shaped *cavatelli.* Buy brands that use a slow-drying method, as indicated by a powdery-looking finish or rough texture, which will help the sauce cling to the pasta.

Stock

Chicken stock, or *brodo di pollo,* is a central component in many of our favorite Italian dishes. We use it to make risotto, to braise poultry and vegetables, and as a base for any number of soups. Store-bought versions work fine, but using stock made from scratch will always yield more sophisticated-tasting results. Simmer chicken parts or carcasses, carrots, onions, and fresh parsley in water until the liquid is deeply flavorful, about 2 hours. Strain and use immediately, or freeze in plastic containers or ice cube trays.

Whole Peeled Tomatoes

Canned tomatoes are workhorses of the Italian kitchen, used for everything from quick, garlicky marinara sauces to long-simmered meat ragùs and vegetable soups. We're partial to organically grown romas from California and also San Marzanos from the Campania region of Italy. Both are plum tomatoes that are meaty and low in moisture, which makes for concentrated, sweet-tasting sauces. Buy whole peeled tomatoes, rather than the diced or crushed kinds, because they're more versatile: You can chop them or squish them by hand to get the desired consistency.

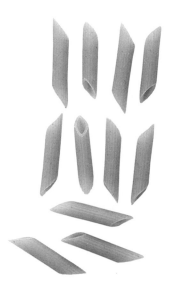

ITALIAN WHITE WINES

Italian wine used to be synonymous with red. But in the past couple decades Italian whites have come of age, and there is now a delicious range of bottles to pair with all sorts of foods. Among our favorites is soave, once a mass-produced table wine. Today's great soaves are fresh and lively with citrus, nut, and steely, spicy mineral flavors. **Soave classico**, from the same-named DOC (*Denominazione di Origine Controllata*) in the calcium-rich volcanic hills surrounding Verona, is terrific with fresh vegetables, pesto, and spicy foods. **Verdicchio** is another white varietal worth trying. Aged verdicchio *riserva* has a golden hue, a velvety texture, and a carmellike richness balanced by a natural acidity. Verdicchios from the Castelli di Jesi DOC, on Le Marche's breezy coast, are a natural match for seafood, while those from the mineral rich soil of Matelica go well with mushroom, truffle, and lighter game dishes. In northern Alto Adige, **pinot bianco**, also called weissburgunder by the region's German speakers, produces medium-bodied wines with floral aromas, green-apple acidity, and a long-lasting finish that pair well with roast pork and cream-based pastas; the region's full-bodied, spicy **traminer**, with hints of lychee and white pepper, also stands up beautifully to rich foods. Another great white wine—particularly with spicy chicken or fish dishes—is the Piedmont's fresh, fruity, honey-nosed **arneis**. In Italy's northeastern corner, Friulian whites range from esoteric varieties like a cidery, amphora-aged style of **vitovska** (great with roasted or cured pork) to the citrusy **pinot grigio** (think antipasti). The Friulian version is the most delicate and flavorful of this variety.

ITALIAN RED WINES

Italy produces more wine than any other nation. Much is rustic, everyday table wine, but there are also legendary reds. Among the most familiar of these is **chianti**, made primarily from Tuscany's sangiovese grape. The star of the variety is full-bodied **chianti classico**, from the heart of the Chianti district, located between Florence and Siena; it has deep notes of black cherry and leather, and is perfect with steak. In the province of Cuneo, southwest of Alba in the Piedmont, the "king of wines," **barolo**, is made in different styles. Traditional barolo is made for aging, with powerful acidity, tannins, and flavors of berry, earth, and tar. Drink it with succulent braised meats. Softer and lusher, younger barolos are great with ragùs and rich risottos, as are jammy **primitivo** wines from Puglia. Hot days, cool nights, and rich volcanic soil lend spicy minerality to grapes grown on Sicily's Mount Etna. **Rosso di Etna** wines go beautifully with swordfish or lamb dishes. From Trentino's sandy Adige valley in the shadow of the Dolomites, the little-known **teroldego rotaliano** has a heady fragrance, lively fruit, and a bitter almond finish that makes a great match for hearty pork or vegetable dishes; the region's plummy, spicy **Lagrein** is also a favorite. Another exciting regional red is Le Marche's **lacrima di Morro d'Alba**, which smells of lavender and tastes of pepper and strawberries; it's wonderful with the region's native truffles and mushrooms. Also great is Veneto's **refosco**—easy to drink and earthy, it's great with pork, poultry, and lamb. And lastly, **sagrantino di Montefalco**, from Umbria, has the tannins that made it suitable for aging, but also an earthiness with lots of fruit that makes it perfect for braised meat sauces.

On the island of Sicily, a local man climbs
the ancient cobblestoned steps.

TABLE OF EQUIVALENTS

The exact equivalents in the following tables have been rounded for convenience.

Liquid and Dry Measurements

U.S.	METRIC
¼ teaspoon	1.25 milliliters
½ teaspoon	2.5 milliliters
1 teaspoon	5 milliliters
1 tablespoon (3 teaspoons)	15 milliliters
1 fluid ounce	30 milliliters
¼ cup	65 milliliters
⅓ cup	80 milliliters
1 cup	235 milliliters
1 pint (2 cups)	480 milliliters
1 quart (4 cups, 32 fluid ounces)	950 milliliters
1 gallon (4 quarts)	3.8 liters
1 ounce (by weight)	28 grams
1 pound	454 grams
2.2 pounds	1 kilogram

Length Measures

U.S.	METRIC
⅛ inch	3 millimeters
¼ inch	6 millimeters
½ inch	12 millimeters
1 inch	2.5 centimeters

Oven Temperatures

FAHRENHEIT	CELSIUS	GAS
250°	120°	½
275°	140°	1
300°	150°	2
325°	160°	3
350°	180°	4
375°	190°	5
400°	200°	6
425°	220°	7
450°	230°	8
475°	240°	9
500°	260°	10

INDEX

ACKNOWLEDGMENTS

Among the many dedicated people who contributed to this book are SAVEUR's executive editor, Dana Bowen, our unofficial mistress of all things Italian; Todd Coleman, executive food editor, who spearheaded not only the recipes in the book but took the majority of the gorgeous photos you see in it; David Weaver, art director extraordinaire; Greg Ferro, our tireless and hilarious managing editor; deputy editors Betsy Andrews and Beth Kracklauer; senior editor, Gabriella Gershenson; research director, Karen Shimizu; assistant editor, Marne Setton; the fabulous test kitchen team of Kellie Evans and Ben Mims and their crackerjack assistants Hilary Merzbacher, Monica Floirendo, Alex Saggiomo, and Victoria Cannizzo; and photo editors Larry Nighswander and Mildred Mattos. We're also grateful to our friends and colleagues at Weldon Owen, including Terry Newell, Hannah Rahill, Jennifer Newens, Amy Marr, Lauren Charles, and Julie Nelson. We'd also like to thank Terry Snow and Jonas Bonnier of Bonnier Corporation for allowing us to have jobs that are so fun that they don't seem like jobs at all. *—James Oseland, Editor-in-Chief*

PHOTOGRAPHY CREDITS

Landon Nordeman 9, 100; **Michael Kraus** 70; **Corbis:** Bettmann, 4; Sabine Lubenow/JAI, 74; all others, **Todd Coleman.**

ISBN 13: 978-1-61628-496-1
ISBN 10: 1-61628-496-X

Design by Dave Weaver

Conceived and produced with SAVEUR by Weldon Owen Inc.
415 Jackson Street, Suite 200, San Francisco, CA 94111
Telephone: 415 291 0100 Fax: 415 291 8841

SAVEUR and Weldon Owen are divisions of **BONNIER**